Lost Cities

by Christopher Fagg

Illustrated by Roger Payne Mike Atkinson Harry Bishop

André Leonard Bryan Evans

Edited by Suzanne le Maitre

Ray Rourke Publishing Company, Inc.
Windermere, Florida 32786

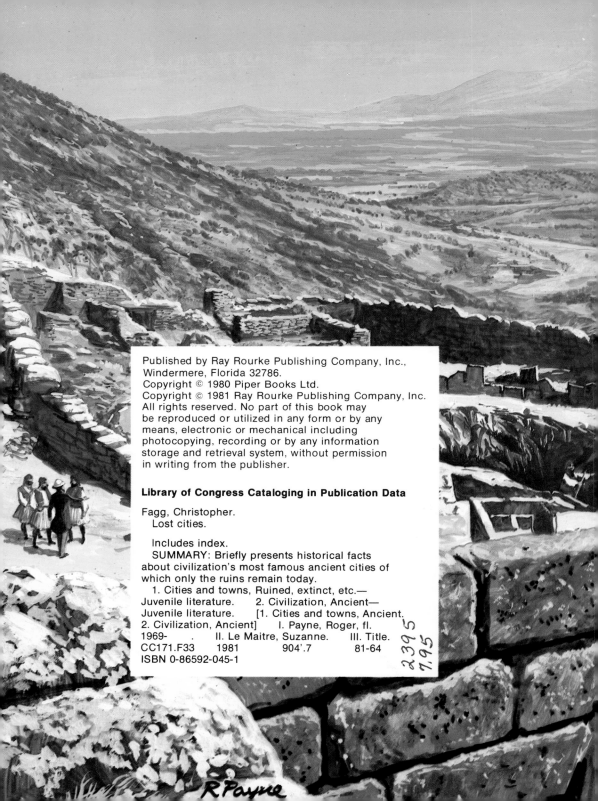

Published by Ray Rourke Publishing Company, Inc.,
Windermere, Florida 32786.

Library of Congress Cataloging in Publication Data

Fagg, Christopher.
  Lost cities.

  Includes index.
  SUMMARY: Briefly presents historical facts
about civilization's most famous ancient cities of
which only the ruins remain today.
  1. Cities and towns, Ruined, extinct, etc.—
Juvenile literature.   2. Civilization, Ancient—
Juvenile literature.   [1. Cities and towns, Ancient.
2. Civilization, Ancient]   I. Payne, Roger, fl.
1969-   .   II. Le Maitre, Suzanne.   III. Title.
CC171.F33   1981   904'.7   81-64
ISBN 0-86592-045-1

2395
1.95

R Payne

Throughout history people have traveled in search of fabled lands and lost cities. With only a few scraps of rumor to go on, explorers have journeyed to the farthest parts of the world. Many have found nothing but disappointment and failure. But if it had not been for the fascination of the unknown, we would still be ignorant of the hidden treasures of the past. In the 19th century, for example, a man called Heinrich Schliemann became obsessed by a single idea. He was sure that the ancient Greek poet Homer held the key to a long-vanished Greek civilization. Homer's long poem the *Iliad* describes a barbaric world of Greek warriors and heroes who attack and burn a great city, Troy. Most people dismissed it as a legend. But Schliemann unearthed the ruins of ancient Troy in Turkey – and went on to make even more important discoveries at Mycenae in Greece. There, amid golden treasures, he found the remains of Greek warrior-kings who ruled more than 3,000 years ago – just as Homer had described them.

Abraham's Birthplace

In the 19th century many archeologists searched for the remains of the lost Bible cities. They unearthed splendid treasures, and as time went on realized that civilization in southern Mesopotamia went back further than the Bible stories. Later, in 1922, an archeologist called Leonard Woolley decided to explore the site of a very ancient city, called Ur of the Chaldees. This Sumerian capital is mentioned in the Bible as the birthplace of Abraham, father of the Hebrew people.

As the excavation progressed Woolley started to uncover the remains of a huge, stepped building, called a *ziggurat*. He managed to gather information about this mysterious monument from the inscriptions around its mud-brick walls. The *ziggurat* had been used as a sacred temple for worship of the moon-god, Nanna.

Six years later, Woolley made an even more amazing discovery. He found an enormous pit filled with dazzling treasure: gold and silver, weapons, musical instruments — and hundreds of human bones. This great death pit was the grave for a king of Ur. His funeral had taken place 3,000 years before Christ was born.

At the ceremony, the king's body was carried into the pit for burial. A procession of his soldiers, palace servants, and sacred oxen, followed behind in mourning. The oxen were slaughtered. Then the followers, standing in orderly ranks, took their own lives — perhaps by poison — to be with their king in death. The pit was filled in, and left undisturbed until Woolley came upon it. But if Ur had not been mentioned in the Bible, this ancient city might have been lost forever.

The retinue of the king lies dying in the great death pit at Ur. It was regarded as a privilege to accompany the king into the next world.

City of Aten

Amun-Ra was the greatest of all the ancient Egyptian gods. In the temples of Thebes, his priests grew rich and powerful through their influence over the ruling kings.

Then in 1379 BC, a new king, Amenhotep IV, came to the throne. He believed that there was only one god, Aten, who showed himself as the disk of the sun. So strong was Amenhotep's belief that he overturned some of Egypt's most sacred traditions, much to his subjects' horror.

He banned all worship of Amun-Ra and the old gods, and ordered a new city to be built in an uninhabited place chosen by Aten – now called Tell el Amarna. His capital was then moved from Thebes to the new city, Akhetaten, about 200 miles to the north. He also changed his name to Akhenaten, to include the name of the one god.

He lived with his beautiful queen, Nefertiti, in the luxury of his new city. But to the dismay of his court and advisers, he neglected his duties in the government in order to worship Aten. After a troubled reign of 20 years, Akhenaten died. The priests took their revenge by moving the court back to Thebes and ordering the destruction of all traces of the dead king's name. The city of Aten was left to decay and the name of Akhenaten accursed forever.

Akhenaten and his beautiful wife Nefertiti worship the one god, Aten, with offerings and sacrifices, in the sacred temple at Akhetaten.

Sacks of grain are brought to be stored in the city granary at Mohenjo-Daro (foreground). The cities of the Indus were well-planned and neatly laid out.

The Indus People

The mighty Indus river flows from Tibet through Pakistan to the Arabian Sea. Vast plains stretch along the valley to the foothills of the Himalayan mountains. These great plains were the site of a long-forgotten civilization that flourished 4,500 years ago.

In the 1920s archeologists began to uncover the ruins of two great cities there, Harappa and Mohenjo-Daro. From what they found, they realized that the Indus valley people had built a civilization to rival those of ancient Mesopotamia and Egypt.

Their wealth was based on farming. In Harappa and Mohenjo-Daro there were huge granaries in which the plentiful grain harvests were stored. They were built on high man-made mounds to protect them from floods, and were run by priests or scribes who used a form of writing that we have not yet been able to decipher.

The cities were laid out in a chessboard pattern of streets with brick houses and shops. Craftsmen made fine jewelry in gold and silver. At the height of their power these cities traded with Mesopotamia, over 1,200 miles away.

For centuries the Indus valley enjoyed prosperity. Then its way of life began to decline. In some places life may have gone on as before. But it is known that Mohenjo-Daro, at least, fell victim to a series of attacks by raiders. How do we know? Because the skeletons of adults and children have been found lying just where they were cut down by the invaders' swords. Flooding, too, may have been a reason for the eventual ruin of the city.

Volcanic explosions on the island of Thera and the resulting tidal waves may have been one of the reasons for the decline of the Cretan civilization.

The Secret Labyrinth

To the ancient Greeks, the island of Crete was a place of mystery and legend. Long ago, they believed, Crete was ruled by the mighty King Minos. One of the most famous stories of Crete was that of the Greek hero Theseus, who traveled to the palace of the King. In a labyrinth, or maze, beneath the palace Theseus met and killed the fearsome Minotaur, a monster that was half man, half bull.

It was not until about a hundred years ago that people began to take legends like this seriously. Could they have been based on fact? Then, in the early 1900s, a British archaeologist called Arthur Evans began to dig at Knossos in northern Crete. There he found the remains of a huge palace. It was a maze of interlocking rooms, corridors, courtyards and flights of steps. As time went on, more palaces and towns were found in Crete — enough to show that a rich and powerful civilization had flourished there 4,000 years ago.

Evans called this civilization "Minoan", after the legendary King. Gradually, we have come to know much more about the Minoans and how they lived. They were traders and seafarers, whose ships sailed to Egypt, Cyprus and the Near East. Their fertile island was rich in grain, olives and wild game, while the surrounding sea teemed with fish. Above all, the Minoans were skilled craftsmen, producing beautiful objects in gold, silver, bronze and painted pottery, which they traded around the Mediterranean.

The Minoans must have felt secure on their island. Their palaces were not fortresses, but centers of a pleasant and easy life. Lively wall paintings show wildlife, dancing and religious ceremonies. Young men and girls are shown leaping gracefully over the backs of huge bulls. Could this game, or ceremony, be connected to the Minotaur story?

The Minoan civilization prospered for centuries, but then, suddenly, it ended. No one knows exactly why the palaces were abandoned in 1450 BC. But a terrible volcanic explosion on the island of Thera, 37 miles away, may have been partly to blame. Earthquakes and tidal waves may have wrecked the Minoan ships and harbors, and destroyed their buildings. Whatever the reason, the glorious days of Crete lived on only in legend.

City of Rock

In the Muslim cemetery in Cairo is a tombstone bearing the name Ibrahim ibn Abdallah. But the man who is buried there was actually a Swiss called John Burckhardt. This extraordinary man spent much of his life exploring the Near East – disguised as a Muslim Arab.

While traveling, Burckhardt heard strange stories of a city hidden in the depths of a mountain in present-day Jordan. He decided to look for it. But the search was not easy. The Arabs in the area distrusted strangers. Finally he persuaded an Arab to lead him there, by telling him that he was on a pilgrimage.

Burckhardt's guide led him down a narrow rocky gorge, over a mile long.

Suddenly it opened out into a valley overshadowed by towering mountains. There, cut into the rock face, were the columns and arches of an ancient city. Burckhardt had rediscovered the city of Petra, lost for a thousand years.

Petra had been the home of the Nabateans, who had developed it into a wealthy trading center. It was a crossroads for caravan routes over the Syrian and Arabian deserts. The city was made a Roman province in AD 106. Many improvements were made by the Romans, including new streets and elegant buildings. But Petra's importance declined as trade routes changed and in AD 636 it fell to Muslim invaders.

A Fiery Death

It was a peaceful summer morning on the Bay of Naples. A string of small towns, and the luxurious villas of rich Romans stretched along the coast. People went about their business, with perhaps no more than a glance at the great volcano, Mount Vesuvius, which overshadowed them. The date was August 24th AD 79.

Suddenly, late in the morning, Vesuvius began to erupt in a series of shattering explosions. The two cities closest to Vesuvius were Pompeii and Herculaneum. Soon after the first blast, ash began to rain down on Pompeii. People fled in panic, streaming out of the city. As the sky grew darker, more and more ash fell, releasing poisonous gases. Many people sheltering in houses and cellars were buried alive as buildings collapsed under the weight of the ash.

Meanwhile, Herculaneum, 9 miles to the west, was overwhelmed by a torrent of volcanic mud – and vanished from sight. By the time the eruption was finally over, Pompeii had almost disappeared under 12 feet of ash.

1,900 years later this ancient disaster has allowed us to see, in fine detail, exactly how these people lived. For archeologists have found houses, streets, shops and their contents preserved under the solidified ash and mud – just as their owners had left them on that fateful day so long ago.

Temple Mountains of Angkor

Deep in the jungles of northern Kampuchea lie the ruins of the vast city of Angkor. Once the capital of the ancient Khmer emperors, this great complex of canals, moats, reservoirs and temples, flourished for over four hundred years.

Emperor Jayavarman II brought his people down from the mountains to farm the fertile plains along the Mekong river in the AD 800s. The Khmers constructed an immense network of canals to control floods and bring water to the rice fields. Angkor was built as a fitting capital to the empire. It was laid out as a great square inside defensive walls. Ceremonial avenues led to a huge open space at the center of the city, overlooked by stone terraces and towers.

Despite its size, few people lived there. It was the sacred home of the Khmer emperors, who were thought of as gods, and their priests and servants. From here they ruled the surrounding countryside.

The greatest glories of Angkor were its colossal temples with rich carvings; they symbolized the mountains from which the emperors' ancestors once spoke to the gods. Each emperor tried to better the one before in the building of his temple-mountain, sometimes demolishing the existing temples to do so.

Most famous of all the temple-mountains is Angkor Wat. Its five towers, pillared galleries and sculptured staircases are covered with thousands of carvings showing scenes from legends and Hindu scriptures.

The last great emperor died in AD 1219. By this time Angkor had become impossible to defend against enemy attacks. Finally the capital was moved and Angkor was left to be swallowed up by the jungle.

The great temple-towers of Angkor Wat rise above terraces and colonnades to dominate an immense reservoir. The whole of Angkor was a ceremonial center for the Khmer god-kings, their priests and servants. Below: A Khmer king at the head of a royal procession. Ceremonies like this were held to ensure fruitful harvests.

When Catherwood and Stephens first saw the Mayan ruins, the ancient temples were choked by jungle growth.

Sacred Cities of the Maya

Long before Europeans set sail for the New World, the Mayan people of Central America ruled a splendid and cruel civilization. From about AD 350 to 700 they built great cities with spacious squares, dominated by temples and shrines set high on pyramid platforms. They invented their own forms of writing and mathematics, and studied the stars and planets. They produced beautifully painted pottery vessels and figures, and wove colored cloth decorated with exotic bird feathers.

The Maya ruled a large area; most of the people were farmers, governed by a small group of priests and officials who lived in the cities. There they held spectacular religious festivals. Many of these ceremonies were savage. One Mayan city called Chichen Itza was built around two sacred wells. Archeologists have discovered skeletons of young girls in the wells, thrown in as sacrifices to the gods together with treasures of gold and jewelry.

Even Mayan games could be a matter of life and death. Many cities had a special court where people played a type of ball game. But this "game" could be played in deadly earnest, with the losing side slaughtered as an offering to the gods.

After centuries of power and greatness the Mayan civilization collapsed. No one can be sure why this happened. It was not until 1839 that two Americans, Frederick Catherwood and John Lloyd Stephens, uncovered the secrets of the Maya. But for the efforts of men like these, the achievements of this brilliant and savage people might still lie undiscovered.

R Payne

Empire of the Sun

In 1911 a young American professor called Hiram Bingham led an expedition to the high Andes mountains of Peru. He was searching for a long-lost city that, according to legend, had been built by Incas fleeing from Spanish invaders. But though many had searched, it had never been found.

For a while it seemed that Bingham's own expedition would fare no better. Then, as he was about to give up, he heard fresh rumors of a ruined mountain city. With only two companions, Bingham set off into the mountains. After a steep climb they rounded a mountain peak – and saw a breathtaking sight.

On top of a great cliff stood a granite fortress. Below it, stretching down the steep mountainside, were layer upon layer of green terraces. This was the lost Inca city of Machu Picchu – built as a last refuge from the gold-hungry Spanish.

Machu Picchu, deserted by its inhabitants only 40 years or so after it was built, was the final achievement of the once mighty Inca empire. During the 1400s and early 1500s the Inca people controlled a huge area stretching southwards along the Andes. They ruled in the name of their sun god – Inti. Rich in gold – which they called "the sweat of the Sun" – the Incas adorned their temples with golden offerings.

But, far away, a Spaniard called Francisco Pizarro heard legends of a kingdom of gold. With a tiny force of 180 men he landed in Peru in 1532. Equipped with firearms, Pizarro's men ruthlessly cut down the Inca armies. The Inca emperor, Atahuallpa, was put to death and soon the Inca empire lay in ruins, its golden treasures plundered.

The Spanish conquistadors slaughter the Incas.

Ghost Towns and Tall Tales

Ghost towns: In this country there were many "ghost towns", places left empty by their former inhabitants. In the gold rushes of the 19th century, mining towns sprang up almost overnight – only to be abandoned when the gold ran out. Virginia City, in the desert state of Nevada, is a famous ghost town. Built during the gold rush of 1859, it was finally deserted in the 1880s.

El Dorado: A legendary city of gold, believed by the Spanish conquistadors to exist somewhere in the Andes mountains of South America. It was said that the Chibcha Indians there had covered their buildings with sheet after sheet of beaten gold for 2,000 years. But the fabulous golden city was never found. It is now thought that El Dorado was a man, not a city – in a ceremony in which the Chibcha chief was covered with powdered gold. The chief was set aboard a raft loaded with gold ornaments and rowed across a sacred lake. There he tossed the ornaments into the water as an offering to the sun god.

Timbuktu: Now a crumbling collection of half-buried buildings on the southern edge of the Sahara Desert. But for 300 years, Timbuktu was a powerful trading city linking North Africa with West Africa. Gold, ivory and slaves were exchanged for salt, dates and metal goods. Tales of the wealth of Timbuktu finally reached Europe, where the name came to stand for all that was romantic and exotic about distant lands.

Atlantis: According to the ancient Greeks, the lost island of Atlantis once existed west of the Pillars of Hercules (Gibraltar). It was eventually swallowed up by the sea. Even in the Middle Ages, 1,500 years later, mapmakers still marked the position of Atlantis on their maps. Its name lives on as that of the ocean which supposedly covers it – the Atlantic Ocean.

Desert sand and wind-blown tumbleweed drift through an abandoned ghost town in the American West.

Index